SEX?

SEX?

EDITED BY MEL CALMAN

Books about SEX
give me
a headache...

INDEX

Published in 1995 by Index
by arrangement with Boxtree Ltd,
Broadwall House, 21 Broadwall, London SE1 9PL

First published in Great Britain in 1993 by
Boxtree Limited

Individual cartoons are copyright of the following:
  © Neil Bennett
  © Mel Calman
  © Heath
  © Tony Husband
  © Larry
  © Ed McLachlan
  © Peattie & Taylor
  © Posy Simmonds
  © Geoff Thompson
  © Kipper Williams
Introduction copyright © Mel Calman 1993

10 9 8 7 6 5 4 3 2 1

ISBN: 1 85283 520 6

Typeset by SX Composing Ltd, Rayleigh, Essex
Printed and bound in Finland by WSOY

A CIP catalogue entry for this book is available from the British Library.

CONTRIBUTORS

Neil Bennett
Mel Calman
Heath
Tony Husband
Larry
Ed McLachlan
Peattie & Taylor
Posy Simmonds
Geoff Thompson
Kipper Williams

How can I write this introduction about SEX, if you keep asking me to come to bed?
Calman

The best way to experience this book is to have a good meal, draw the curtains, light the candles, put some romantic music on the CD player, change into something comfortable and enjoy yourself.

And if the book is not all you hoped for, you needn't tell anybody.

Mel Calman

"Not this year, darling — I've got a headache"

"AND OF COURSE IT'S FULL OF
SEXUAL INNUENDO."

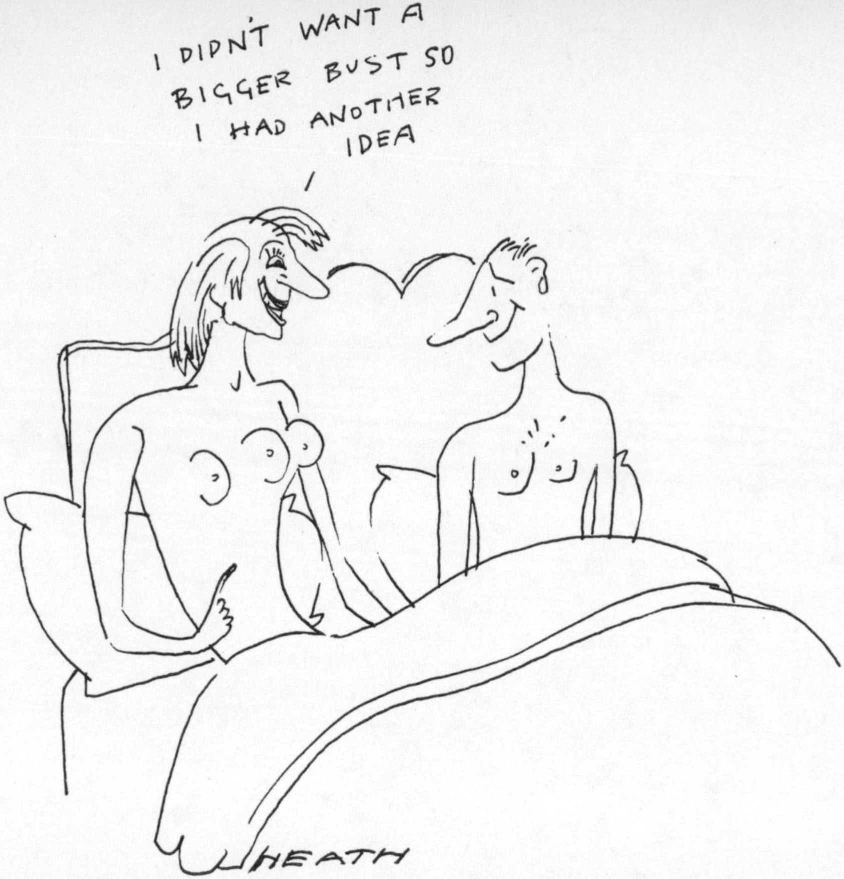
I DIDN'T WANT A BIGGER BUST SO I HAD ANOTHER IDEA
HEATH

PILLOW TALK

'I know you went to a prep school, Hugh, but you don't have to write a thank-you letter every time we make love.'

'I'LL BE GLAD WHEN
CHRISTMAS IS OVER'

"NOT AGAIN!"

"I bet they had more fun conceiving me than you!"

" I must speak seriously to Mellors."

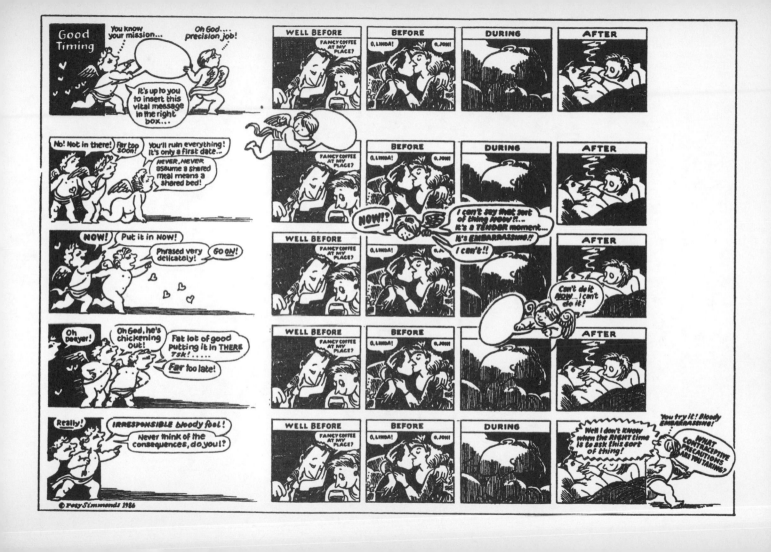

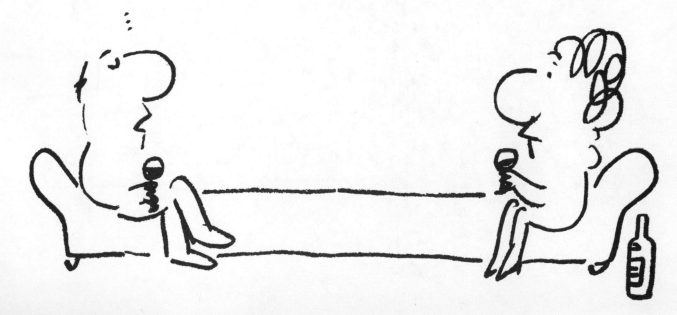

"And then there are some things you don't need to know till you're Henry IV Part 2."

for goodness sake -
it has to be BOOTS -
wellies won't do ..

"Well, hi there!"

"Even after all these years you're still very uptight about sex, aren't you Phillip?"

"Can we dispense with foreplay tonight dear?"

"YOU ONLY WANT ME
FOR MY BODY."

Geoff Thompson

"Dear Sun Editor, I have just seen the first cuckold of spring!"

"Phew, you wait ages for one and three come together!"

" I'd like to defer having a family until I reach a career plateau."

McLACHLAN

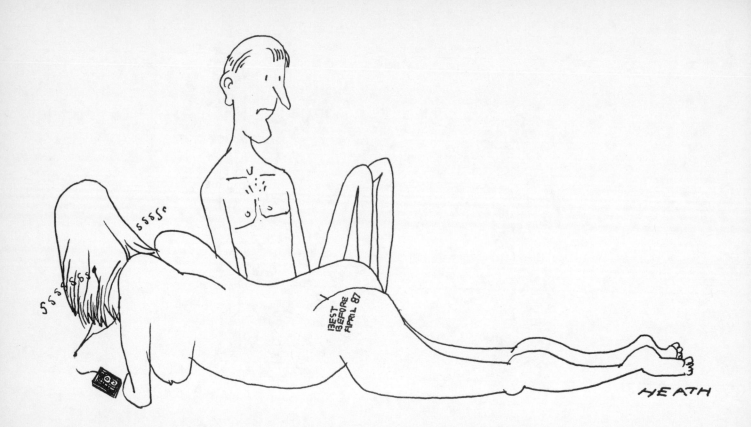

"Julian — I have been less than frank with you"

"Penny for your thoughts, dear."

TRUE PRIDE

Right Reverend Host. " I CANNOT ALLOW YOU TO MARRY MY DAUGHTER,
MR. JONES. YOUR STIPEND IS TOO SMALL!"

The Curate. "OH NO, MY LORD, I ASSURE YOU! THOUGH THE END
BE SMALL PARTS OF IT ARE EXCELLENT!"

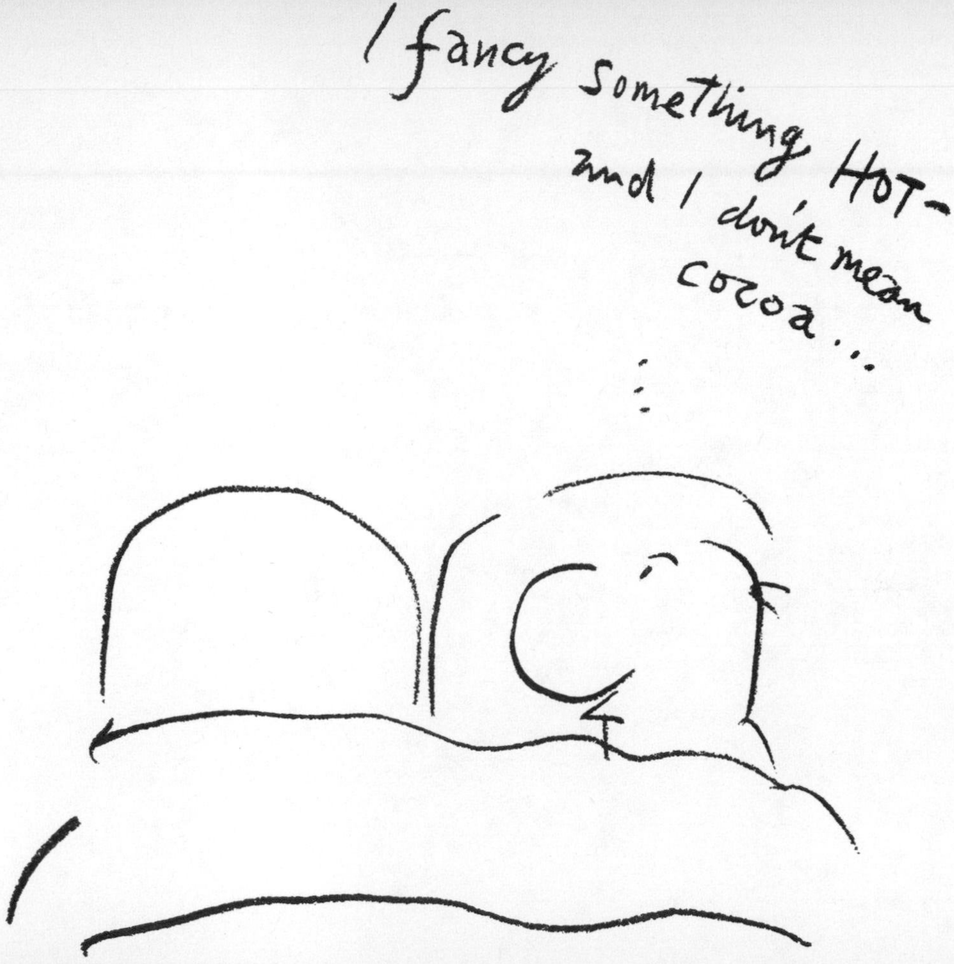
I fancy something HOT-
and I don't mean
cocoa...

Any time you want me
to drive you into the arms
of another woman —
please let me know!

Here I am, an erstwhile victim of **FLAB** and *middle-aged* **TORPOR**,...having pulled my **socks** up...

...Having given up *starch, sugar, ciggies & scotch*...having just lost **2 stone** & found a **waist**...having lowered my *cholesterol* count & improved **muscle tone**....

...having discovered that one's **stomach** is only so big...like a little **bowl**....

...having begun the day with a glass of *hot water* & 20 press ups...having lunched on 2 spoonfuls of **BRAN** & a *green salad*...having dined on *spinach* & **Malvern** water....,

© Posy Simmonds 1980

GURGLE LURGLE·GLOOGLE LOOOOGLE! GURGLE LURGLE LURGLE

"WE'RE TRYING TO HELP MISS WODEHILL, SIR. TRACY OVERHEARD HER SAY SHE LOST HER VIRGINITY LAST NIGHT."

McLACHLAN

I don't mind you wearing my dress— but I do mind you getting more WOLF whistles in it...

I had him as a *kitten*...he was a stray...
.. I had him *neutered* and all that......
I think he's *SAGGITARIUS*....

For her, I gave up my freedom, my independance & my chances of fatherhood!

But *right now*, he's *SCREWING UP* my life and my *relationship!!* What do I do with him?

For 5 years I've been her faithful, live-in, domestic companion...

And now she's getting hitched to that *wimp, Michael!!! £?**!*

He's jealous of your fiancé, that's all...

Five years she's been my mistress!!

© PosySimmonds

Poor Mr Tibbles! Look, he's almost human! Aaah... if he could talk, he would! Tell me what you want, Pussy....

Palimony!

SAFE SEX

McLACHLAN

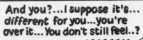

© Posy Simmonds 1986

" I must say I find the introverts less threatening."

"Oh God! It's my husband!"

"Hello, tailor."

"Incredible! How was it for you?"

"IT'S ALL OVER. I'VE FOUND SOMEONE ELSE."

"I like you Thompson. I like your drive, ambition, but mostly I like your cute bottom."

"I'VE GOT YOU FIXED UP AS WELL, HE'S BRINGING HIS BEST FRIEND ALONG"

"YOU MARRY THEM FOR THEIR COME-TO-BED-EYES
AND YOU END UP WITH GONE-TO-BED-EYES."

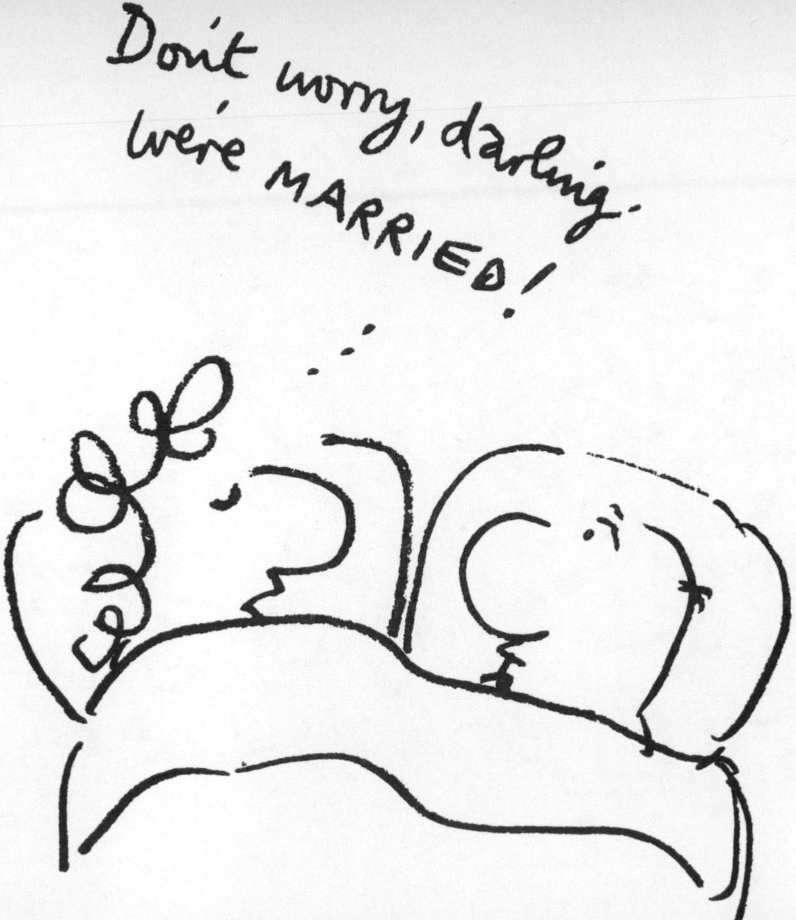
Don't worry, darling. We're MARRIED!

"My son was right . . . you've got great boobs."

When I said I'd like to make LOVE to two women – I didn't think you'd send for your MOTHER...

'HOW DO I LOVE THEE, LET ME COUNT THE WAYS!'